D0676520

A MOMENT'S PEACE

❧

A MOMENT'S PEACE

❖

Words of Encouragement

POPE JOHN PAUL II

CH*A*RIS

Servant Publications
Ann Arbor, Michigan

© 1984, 1987, 1995 by the K.S. Giniger Company, Inc. All rights reserved.

Charis Books is an imprint of Servant Publications especially designed to serve Roman Catholic readers.

Previously published as *Pope John Paul II, Pilgrim of Faith*. © 1987, 1984 by the K.S. Giniger Company, Inc.

Published by Servant Publications
P.O. Box 8617
Ann Arbor, Michigan 48107

Cover design by Diane Bareis
Cover photo: Westlight
Cover photo, Pope John Paul II: Bettmann

    96 97 98 99 10 9 8 7 6 5 4 3

Printed in the United States of America
ISBN 0-89283-966-X

"With firm faith,
renewed hope,
and ever deeper love."

✤

Pope John Paul II

A moment's peace...

We all want it. We need it every day. But in our frenetic, busy, and sometimes troubled lives, we don't always find it.

If you are looking for spiritual refreshment—a breath of fresh air amid the turmoil of your daily routine—pause and read a bit of *A Moment's Peace*. You will find encouragement in these words of Pope John Paul II. These short excerpts from the pope's writings will speak to you of matters close to your heart. He writes to you about love, faith, hope, joy, peace, family, and unity.

Let this pope who has done so much to advance the cause of peace in the world advance the cause of peace in your heart.

❖

Messages
of Faith

❖

We Are All Pilgrims

*N*othing can give us a profound sense of the meaning of our earthly life and stimulate us to live it as a brief experimental state—as can an inner *attitude of seeing ourselves as pilgrims.*

*I*n Christ, religion is no longer a blind search for God, but the response of faith to God who reveals Himself. It is a response in which man speaks to God as his Creator and Father, a response made possible by that one Man, [Christ].

*I*t is not enough to accept passively those riches of the faith which are handed down in your tradition and by your culture. A treasure is entrusted, talents are offered, which ought to be accepted with responsibility, so that they may bear fruit in abundance.

*T*o believe means to abandon oneself to the truth of the word of the living God, knowing and humbly recognizing [as St. Paul says] "how unsearchable are His judgments and how inscrutable His ways."

*M*ary said: "I am the servant of the Lord. Let it be done to me as you say" (Lk 1:38). And, with these words, she expressed what was *the fundamental attitude of her life: her faith*. Mary believed! She trusted in God's promises and was faithful to His will. All her earthly life was a "pilgrimage of faith." For, like us, she walked in shadows and hoped for things unseen....

*Y*ou receive the gift of the Holy Spirit so that you may work with deep faith and with abiding charity, so that you may help bring to the world the fruits of reconciliation and peace.

*We live our faith
when we are open to God's coming,
when we persevere in His advent.*

❧ ⚜ ❧

*T*he attitude of spirit befitting the believer is an attitude of vigilance, the expression of spiritual aspiration to God through faith.

*E*ducation in the faith by parents...is already being given when the members of a family help each other to grow in faith through the witness of their Christian lives, a witness that is often without words but which perseveres throughout a day-to-day life lived in accordance with the Gospel.

*A*lways have the courage and pride of your faith. Deepen it. *Get close to Christ, ceaselessly,* as living stones in the cornerstone, sure of reaching the goal of your faith, the salvation of your souls.

Faith in a Difficult Age

We have so much need of faith! Great faith is so necessary to men of our time, the difficult modern age. Great faith is necessary today to individual families, communities, the Church.

*T*his epoch of ours requires from us Christians: "Faith plain to see and courageous, faith full of hope, faith living through love."

*T*he most valuable gift that the Church can offer to the bewildered and restless world of our time is to form within it Christians who are confirmed in what is most essential [to faith] and who are humbly joyful in their faith.

[O ur faith must be] translated into
lifestyle according to the
Gospel,... a way of living which reflects
the Beatitudes, shows itself in love, as the
key to human existence, and adds power
to the values of the person, to commit
the person to solving the human problems of our time.

*O*ur daily lives are in danger of experiencing—actually do experience—cases of inner pollution. But contact in faith with the word of the Lord purifies us, elevates us, and gives us back energy.

*O*nly he who accepts his intellectual and moral *limits* and recognizes that he *needs* salvation can attain to faith and in faith meet, in Christ, his Redeemer.

*F*aith… in its relation with culture pre-sents itself as a clarification of God's project, as an aid and complement to rationality. But rationality is not im-poverished by having recourse to the Faith.

*S*cience and faith are both gifts of God....The light of reason, which makes science possible, and the light of Revelation, which makes faith possible, emanate from a single Source.

*I*f we look at today's world, we are struck by many negative factors that can lead to pessimism. But this feeling is unjustified: We have faith in God our Father and Lord, in His goodness and mercy....God is preparing a great springtime for Christianity, and we can already see its first signs.

I wish to invite the Church to renew her missionary commitment....For missionary activity renews the Church, revitalizes faith and Christian identity, and offers fresh enthusiasm and new incentive. Faith is strengthened when it is given to others!

To Those Who Struggle

*L*ike Jesus Christ, truth may always be denied, persecuted, embattled, wounded, martyred, crucified; but it always lives again and rises again and cannot be wrenched out of the human heart.

*T*he reality of faith, of hope, and of charity, the reality of suffering sanctified and sanctifying, the reality of the presence of the mother of God in the mystery of Christ and His Church on earth are a presence which is particularly alive in... the sick and the suffering.

*A*part from faith, pain has always been a great riddle of human existence. Ever since Jesus redeemed the world by His passion and death, however, a new perspective has been opened: Through suffering one can grow in self-giving and attain the highest degree of love....because of Him who "loved us and gave Himself for us."

I thank God for the lives
of all those who, wherever they be,
suffer for their faith in God.

⚜ ⚜ ⚜

Look with the Eyes of Faith

*L*et us look now with "the eyes of faith" to Christ's kingdom, and repeat, "May Your reign come."

*T*he more man lets himself be carried away by the eloquence of creatures, their richness and beauty, the more the need to adore the Creator grows in him.

Genuine faith:
It is absolute dedication
to things which are not seen,
but which are capable
of filling and ennobling a whole life.

⚜ ⚜ ⚜

*F*rom the outset, conversion is expressed in faith which is total and radical, and which neither limits nor hinders God's gift.... Conversion means accepting, by a personal decision, the saving sovereignty of Christ and becoming His disciple.

*T*he ways of knowledge [are] through faith, for only such knowledge of the faith disposes the understanding to *union with the living God.*

*G*od the Father's plan of salvation embraces all mankind; His one same Holy Spirit is sent as a gift to all who are open to receive Him in faith.

The soul—
the more it will have faith,
so much the more will it
be united to God.

I exhort you to be courageous now and always, without becoming bewildered by difficulties, and always trusting in Him who is your Friend and your Redeemer, and watching and praying to keep your faith sound and your grace lively.

*P*ause and give thanks to God for the unique culture and rich human tradition which you have inherited and for the greatest gift anyone can receive, the gift of faith.

PRAYER

✤ ✤ ✤

We ask Almighty God to renew the face of the earth through the life-giving power of the Spirit. Send forth Your Spirit, O Lord, renew our hearts and minds with the gifts of light and truth. Renew Your Church on earth with the gifts of penance and reconciliation, with unity in faith and love.

*T*his woman of faith, Mary of Nazareth, the mother of God, has been given to us as *a model in our pilgrimage of faith*. From Mary, we learn to surrender to God's will in all things.

Messages
of Hope

Everything Is New!

When you meet Christ in prayer, when you get to know His Gospel and reflect on it in relation to your hopes and your plan for the future, then everything is new.

*I*n the cross lies hope of a Christian renewal,... but only if Christians themselves take the message of the cross seriously.

*T*he Lord is always with you... to give all the regenerative power of His Gospel, of His grace, and of His love. Never ignore Him! Never put Him aside!

*C*hrist rose again so that man may retrieve the authentic meaning of existence, *so that man may live his life fully;* that man, who comes *from God,* may live *in God*.

What is the truth which penetrates and enlivens us today? What message does the Church, our Mother, announce? The message of hope.

*C*hanged by the working of grace into a new creature, the Christian... humbly sets himself to follow Christ and learns more and more within the Church to think like Him, to judge like Him, to act in conformity with His commandments, and to hope as He invites us to.

*P*rayer is not one occupation among many, but is at the center of our life in Christ. It turns our attention away from ourselves and directs it to the Lord. Prayer fills the mind with truth and gives hope to the heart.

*H*ope, on the one hand, encourages the Christian not to lose sight of the final goal which gives meaning and value to life; and on the other, offers solid and profound reasons for a daily commitment to God's plan.

*B*ehold the day of universal hope, the day on which all human sufferings, disappointments, humiliations, crosses, violated human dignity, disrespected human life, all are gathered up and associated with the Risen One.

*T*he Spirit is given to the Church in order that through His power the whole community of the People of God, however widely scattered and diverse, may persevere in hope: that hope in which "we have been saved." It is the hope of definitive fulfillment in God, the hope of the eternal Kingdom.

Be Heralds of Hope!

*M*en and women of deep and abiding faith: Be heralds of hope. Be messengers of joy. Be true workers for justice.

*T*his is the certainty of which the world had need, the world in which the apostles preached the Gospel of Christ; this is the hope of Him of whom humanity in our time has need, those to whom we would communicate the message: Christ is risen, and by rising again He has broken what seemed and still seems to many an implacable vortex of decadence, degradation, and corruption in history.

*T*hey live without true joy because they live without hope. They live without hope because they have never heard, really heard, the Good News of Jesus Christ, because they have never met a brother or a sister who touched their lives with the love of Jesus and lifted them up from their misery.

*P*rayer becomes a need of the soul: "In prayer the heart alters and in this conversion the inner eye becomes pure." Pray in hope, pray with faith and love. Prayer is as necessary as the grace it obtains for us.

We must... become more and more united with Christ, therefore more united among ourselves in Christ. He alone... can bring our hopes to fulfillment.

Deep truth [is] truth which
converts, restores hope,
puts everything in its place,
reconciles and lets optimism arise.

⚜ ⚜ ⚜

*I*ndispensable to today's diplomacy is... the ever deeper insertion of the supreme values of the moral and spiritual order into the aims of peoples and into the methods used in pursuit of these aims.

*Only through acceptance
of the Gospel can every
hope... find full realization.*

❧ ❧ ❧

"*P*eace I leave with you; my peace I give to you," Christ has said to us. This divine promise fills us with the hope, indeed the certainty of divine hope, that peace is possible, because nothing is impossible with God.

Death has its limits.
Christ has opened up a great hope:
the hope of life beyond
the sphere of death.

❦ ⚜ ❦

Our Light of Hope

*H*ave humble and courageous awareness of what the Father has given you. Let this awareness be your strength, your light, your hope.

*T*he divine wisdom is that *sublime science* which preserves the savor of salt, so that it will not become tasteless: which feeds the light of the lamp, so that it may light up the depths of the human heart, guide its secret yearnings, its seeking, and its hopes.

*F*aith, based on the Gospel story, tells us that God became man. That is, He entered into human history not so much to challenge it as to *enlighten* it, to *orient* it, to *save* it, by redeeming every single soul. This is the meaning of the Incarnation of the Word; this is the authentic meaning of Christmas, the feast of true joy and true hope. May the light of hope reveal itself to all.

*I*n spite of all, there is hope and joy because God became man, because Christ was really incarnated for us, the Savior announced by the prophets came, and has remained with us!

With the Church's liturgy,
we may greet the cross as
"the only hope" and source
of grace and pardon.

❧ ❧ ❧

*M*ary is a living word of comfort for the Church in her struggle.... As we, the pilgrim people... make our way in confidence towards a "new heaven and new earth," we look to her who is for us "a sign of sure hope and solace."

PRAYER

✤ ✤ ✤

Lord, may Your grace be upon us,
because we hope in You.

✦

Messages
of Love

✦

God's Constant Love

What really matters in life is that we are loved by Christ and that we love Him in return. In comparison with the love of Jesus, everything else is secondary. And, without the love of Jesus, everything else is useless.

*I*f God goes in search of man, created in His own image and likeness, He does so because He loves him eternally in the Word, and wishes to raise him in Christ to the dignity of an adopted son.

*I*t is exactly this God,... the Creator and Redeemer, who makes the profession of such love for man, for man the sinner: "Though the mountains leave their place, and the hills be shaken, my love shall never leave you" (Is 54:10).

*T*he more we purify our souls, the more shall we make room for God's love in our hearts, the more Christ will be able to come and be born in us!

*J*esus Christ is a "King who loves" because He loved us humans to the shedding of His blood. Because He loves, He has liberated us from sin, because only love is capable of freeing us from sin.

*O*nly love creates good and, in the last analysis, it alone can be perceived in all dimensions and profiles in created things and in man above all.

We must measure man according to the gauge of the conscience, with the measure of the spirit open to God. Only the Holy Spirit can fill up this heart, that is, lead it to self-realization through love and wisdom.

Blessed be God, rich in mercy,
for the great love with which
He has loved us!

⚜ ⚜ ⚜

*W*ithout a healthy awareness of their own sinfulness, people will never experience the depth of God's redeeming love for them while they were still sinners.

We Are Called to Love

*G*od created man in His image and likeness by calling him into existence *for love's sake;* at the same time He called him *to love.* God is love and lives a mystery of personal communion of love in Himself.... Love is the fundamental and native vocation of every human being.

*C*reating the human race in His own image...God inscribed in the humanity of man and woman the vocation, and thus the capacity and responsibility, of love and communion.

*T*here are always souls to enlighten, sinners to pardon, tears to dry, disappointments to console, sick to encourage, children and youngsters to guide. There is, there ever shall be, man to love and save, in Christ's name!

*M*an lives in the full dimension of his humanity only when he is capable of *surpassing himself with the power of truth and love.*

We receive the Holy Spirit, that the power of truth and love may form our interior life and make it radiate outwardly as well.

A Christian who has not learned to see and love Christ in his neighbor is not fully Christian. We are our brothers' keepers; we are bound to each other by the bond of love.

We must love others with the same love
which God pours into our hearts
and with which He
Himself loves us.

⚜ ⚜ ⚜

*Love which is directed to man
actually always finds its ultimate source
in God, who is love.*

⚜ ⚜ ⚜

*T*he vocation to love, understood as a true openness to our fellow human beings and solidarity with them, is the most basic of all vocations. It is the origin of all vocations in life.

*E*arthly suffering, when accepted in love, is like a bitter kernel containing the seed of new life, the treasure of divine glory to be given man in eternity.

*S*o many problems arise when people think of the Church as "theirs," when in fact she belongs to Christ. Christ and the Church are inseparably united as "one flesh" (see Eph 5:31). Our love for Christ finds its vital expression in our love for the Church.

Mary, Mother of beautiful love, pray for us! Teach us to love God and our brethren, as you have loved them. Cause our love for others to be ever patient, benign, respectful.

Love Can Change the World

*B*elieving in the crucified Son means "seeing the Father," means believing that love is present in the world and that this love is more powerful than any kind of evil in which individuals, humanity, or the world is involved.

*M*ercy is an indispensable dimension of love; it is, as it were, love's second name and, at the same time, the specific manner in which love is revealed and effected vis-à-vis the reality of the evil that is in the world.

*T*he message of the Beatitudes [is] the message of love for God and one's neighbor, the message of moral commitment to the authentic transformation of society.

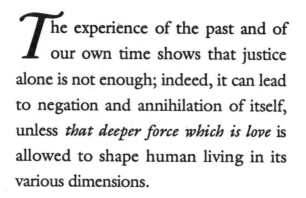

*T*he experience of the past and of our own time shows that justice alone is not enough; indeed, it can lead to negation and annihilation of itself, unless *that deeper force which is love* is allowed to shape human living in its various dimensions.

*T*he vocation to holiness must be recognized and lived by the lay faithful... as an undeniable and demanding obligation and as a shining example of the infinite love of the Father that has regenerated them in His own life of holiness.

*S*ay "No" to death, to hatred, to violence, to terror, to error, to evil, to degradation. Say "Yes" to the good, to the beautiful, to truth, to justice, to responsibility, to life, to peace, to love.

*G*enuine understanding and compassion must mean love for the person, for his true good, for his authentic freedom. And this does not result, certainly, from concealing or weakening moral truth, but rather from proposing it in its most profound meaning as an outpouring of God's eternal wisdom.

A charity that loves and serves the person is never able to be separated from justice. Each in its own way demands the full, effective acknowledgement of the rights of the individual to which society is ordered in all its structures and institutions.

*T*he Gospel... urges us *to share every one of man's situations and conditions,* with a passionate love for everything to do with his condition of being a creature of God's.

*P*rayer not only opens us up to a meeting with the Most High but also disposes us to a meeting with our neighbor, helping us to establish with everyone, without discrimination, relationships of respect, understanding, esteem, and love.

*T*he Eucharist educates us to... love in a deeper way; it shows us, in fact, what value each person, our brother or sister, has in God's eyes, if Christ offers Himself equally to each one, under the species of bread and wine.

*L*ove... mankind,... all mankind, without any exception or division at all: without difference of race, of culture, of language, of concept of the world, without distinction between friends and enemies. This is love for mankind and it desires every true good for each member of mankind.

The deepest spring of man's spiritual development is found in the evangelical commandment of love.

❧ ❧ ❧

*L*et us persevere in asking the Holy Spirit to remove all divisions from our faith, to give us the perfect unity in truth and love for which Christ prayed, for which Christ died.

*H*ave the courage to present Christ!... Helping a brother or sister to discern Christ, the Way, the Truth, and the Life, is a true act of love for one's neighbor.

*L*ove and life according to the Gospel cannot be thought of first and foremost as a kind of precept, because what they demand is beyond man's abilities. They are possible only as the result of a gift of God who heals, restores, and transforms the human heart by His grace.

A Touch of Eternal Love

*T*he cross is like a touch of eternal love upon the most painful wounds of man's earthly existence.

*T*he whole of the Christian life is like a great pilgrimage to the house of the Father, whose unconditional love for every human creature...we discover anew each day.

*O*ur reconciliation with God, the return to the Father's house, is accomplished through Christ. His suffering and death on the cross stand between every human conscience, every human sin, and the Father's boundless love. Such love is prompt to rise up and pardon; it is nothing else than mercy.

*G*od's salvation is the work of a love greater than man's sin. Love alone can wipe out sin and liberate from sin. Love alone can consolidate man in the good, in the unalterable and eternal good.

*T*he world and man *were consecrated through the power of the redemption.* They were consecrated to Him who is infinitely holy. They were offered and confided to Love Himself, to the merciful Love.

*E*very epoch—past, present, and to come—produces shining examples of the power which is in Jesus Christ for the edification of all... to give testimony of the primacy of love in the world.

*T*here is a pledge of satisfaction for that burning thirst for happiness and love which everyone bears in himself and herself, in the secret of the heart.

The Blessings of Married Love

*L*ove is not a passing emotion—a temporary infatuation—but a responsible and free decision to bind oneself completely, "in good times and in bad," to one's partner... the gift of oneself to the other.

118

*C*onjugal love entails a totality where all components of the person, the claims of the body and of the instincts, the power of feeling and affection, the aspirations of the spirit and of the will, all enter in. It aims at a profoundly personal unity, that which goes beyond union in one flesh and leads to making but one heart and one soul.

*S*exuality is realized in a truly human way only if it is an integral part of the love with which the man and the woman commit themselves to each other until death.

*L*ove, reinforced by the grace of the sacrament of matrimony, shall show itself to be stronger than any weakness and every crisis through which our families pass....

*I*n its deepest reality, love is essentially giving and, while conjugal love leads the spouses to reciprocal "knowledge" which makes them "one flesh," it does not end within the couple; it makes them capable of the greatest possible giving whereby they become cooperators with God for the gift of life and a new human person.

To Families

*T*he parents' love... [inspires and guides] the whole of the concrete work of education, and enriching it with those values of gentleness, constancy, goodness, service, and spirit of sacrifice, which are the most precious fruit of love.

*P*arental love is called to become the visible sign to the children of God's own love, that of Him "from whom all fatherhood in heaven and on earth is named."

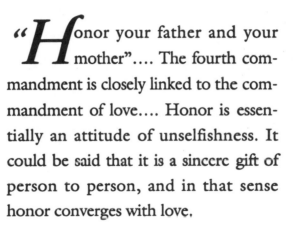

"*H*onor your father and your mother".... The fourth commandment is closely linked to the commandment of love.... Honor is essentially an attitude of unselfishness. It could be said that it is a sincere gift of person to person, and in that sense honor converges with love.

*T*he Church sees in the face of women the reflection of a beauty which mirrors the loftiest sentiments of which the human heart is capable: the self-offering totality of love; the strength that is capable of bearing the greatest sorrows; the limitless fidelity and tireless devotion to work; the ability to combine penetrating intuition with words of support and encouragement.

PRAYER

Jesus Christ, Son of the Living God, grant that... all of us may love You more, as in ourselves we live the mysteries of Your life again, from the conception and birth up to the cross and the resurrection.